Ten P[oems]
about Tea

ex libris

Helen
Lockett

Candlestick Press

Published by:
Candlestick Press,
DiVersity House, 72 Nottingham Road,
Arnold, Nottingham NG5 6LF
www.candlestickpress.co.uk

Design, typesetting, print and production by DiVersity Creative
Marketing Solutions Ltd., www.diversity-nottm.co.uk

Illustrations: © Jill Perry www.jillperry.com, 2011
Introduction: © Sophie Dahl, 2011

© Candlestick Press, 2011

ISBN 978 1 907598 02 9

Acknowledgements:
Candlestick Press wishes to thank Sophie Dahl for her generous
contribution to *Ten Poems about Tea*. Thanks are also due to Lorraine
Mariner, who came up with the idea and supplied us with the poems.
We raise a steaming tea-cup to them both.

Poems are reprinted by kind permission of Tiffany Atkinson and
Seren Books for 'Tea' (from *Kink and Particle*, Seren Books, 2007);
Carol Ann Duffy and Macmillan Publishers Ltd for 'Tea' (from
Rapture, Picador, 2005); Tim Arlott for John Arlott, 'Tea with
my Aunts'; Kenny Knight and Shearsman Books for 'Lessons in
Teamaking' (from The *Honicknowle Book of the Dead*, Shearsman
Books, 2009); Eavan Boland and Carcanet Press for 'In Season'
(from *Domestic Violence*, Carcanet Press, 2007). 'In a Bath Teashop'
© John Betjeman is reprinted by permission of The Estate of John
Betjeman. Our thanks also to John Agard and Bloodaxe Books for
permission to reprint 'Alternative Anthem' (from *Selected Poems*,
Bloodaxe Books, 2008) and to Jo Shapcott and Faber and Faber Ltd
for 'Procedure' (from *Of Mutability*, Faber and Faber, 2010).

Where poets are no longer living, their dates are given.

Introduction

The ritual of tea is one I've always loved. As a child, I held tea parties for my dolls, and the brilliant thing I discovered about dolls, was that they didn't really eat or drink, which meant all the more tea for me. As I got older, the tea parties became a bit less one sided, and I learnt that tea always has a language, never more potent than in the "How do you take it?" early days of courtship.

Carol Ann Duffy says it best, with her "I like the questions – sugar? milk? / And the answers I don't know by heart, yet / For I see your soul in your eyes and I forget".

How well I remember the morning cups of half-drunk PG, or English Breakfast, the afternoon tempered with a weak sugarless Earl Grey and a biscuit. The things that become second nature in tender dog-eared togetherness which early on feel like the discoveries of Columbus in miniature.

When I was very young I had a boyfriend from up North, with nice sensible parents who regarded my family as some sort of anthropological curiosity. One day, with nothing better to do, the boyfriend's mum and I were discussing a particularly mad relative, who no doctor seemed able to cure. "Tell you what our kid," she breathed into the phone, taking another suck on her Mayfair Super King, "There's nowt that won't cure that woman like a walk round the lakes, a fair old chat, and a good strong cup of tea." Thing is, she was probably right.

"Tea is drunk to forget the din of the world" the Chinese scholar Tien Yiheng said, and he was right. For love and madness and everything that sandwiches in between, a cup of tea can set the world softly back to rights.

Sophie Dahl (PG with milk, no sugar)

Tea

I like pouring your tea, lifting
the heavy pot, and tipping it up,
so the fragrant liquid steams in your china cup.

Or when you're away, or at work,
I like to think of your cupped hands as you sip,
as you sip, of the faint half-smile of your lips.

I like the questions – sugar? milk? –
and the answers I don't know by heart, yet,
for I see your soul in your eyes, and I forget.

Jasmine, Gunpowder, Assam, Earl Grey, Ceylon,
I love tea's names. Which tea would you like? I say,
but it's any tea, for you, please, any time of day,

as the women harvest the slopes,
for the sweetest leaves, on Mount Wu-Yi,
and I am your lover, smitten, straining your tea.

Carol Ann Duffy

In a Bath Teashop

"Let us not speak, for the love we bear one another –
    Let us hold hands and look."
She, such a very ordinary little woman;
    He, such a thumping crook;
But both, for a moment, little lower than the angels
    In the teashop's ingle-nook.

John Betjeman (1906 - 1984)

At Tea

The kettle descants in a cosy drone,
And the young wife looks in her husband's face,
And then at her guest's, and shows in her own
Her sense that she fills an envied place;
And the visiting lady is all abloom,
And says there was never so sweet a room.

And the happy young housewife does not know
That the woman beside her was first his choice,
Till the fates ordained it could not be so....
Betraying nothing in look or voice
The guest sits smiling and sips her tea,
And he throws her a stray glance yearningly.

Thomas Hardy (1840 - 1928)

Lessons in Teamaking

When I first learned to
pour tea in Honicknowle

in those dark old days
before central heating

closed down open fireplaces
and lights went out in coal mines

and chimpanzees hadn't yet
made their debuts on television

and two sugars
was the national average

and the teapot was the centre
of the known universe

and the sun was this yellow
thing that just warmed the air

and anthropology's study
of domestic history hadn't

quite reached the evolutionary
breakthrough of the tea bag

and the kettle was on
in the kitchen of

number thirty two Chatsworth Gardens
where my father after slurping

another saucer dry would ask
in a smoke-frog voice for

another cup of microcosm
while outside the universe blazed

like a hundred towns
on a sky of smooth black lino

and my father with tobacco
stained fingers would dunk biscuits

and in the process spill tiny drops
of Ceylon and India

which I would wipe with a tea towel
from the corner shop

I read the tea leaves
as if they were words

left over from a conversation
between two cups.

Kenny Knight

Tea

You made me tea
while I shook the rain from my jacket.
You stooped to fit into the kitchen,
but handled the cups as if they'd been
the fontanelles of two young sons
whose picture sits in the hip of your 501s.
We spoke of – what? Not much.
You weren't to know how your touch
with the teaspoon stirred me,
how the tendons of your wide, divining hands
put me in mind of flight.

You wouldn't have known
when you bent to tend a plant
that your shirt fell open a smile's breadth.
You parted the leaves and plucked
a tiny green bud. Best to do that
with the early ones, you said.
I thought of the salt in the crook
of your arm where a fine vein kicks.
Of what it might be like to know
the knot and grain and beat of you;
the squeak of your heart's pips.

Tiffany Atkinson

Alternative Anthem

Put the kettle on
Put the kettle on
It is the British answer
to Armageddon.

Never mind taxes rise
Never mind trains are late
One thing you can be sure of
and that's the kettle, mate.

It's not whether you lose
It's not whether you win
It's whether or not
you've plugged the kettle in.

May the kettle ever hiss
May the kettle ever steam
It is the engine
that drives our nation's dream.

Long live the kettle
that rules over us
May it be limescale free
and may it never rust.

Sing it on the beaches
Sing it from the housetops
The sun may set on empire
but the kettle never stops.

John Agard

Tea with my Aunts

Tea with my aunts at half-past four,
Tea in a world without a war;
The Widow-Queen is still alive
In grandpa's house in Albert Drive,
And firm the monkey-puzzle tree
He planted at the Jubilee.

A frilly, fragile cup of tea
Unsafely balanced on my knee,
Aunt Anna mellows as I take
Another slice of home-made cake,
She rustles in her stiff grey gown
And takes her endless knitting down.

A chastely-ringed and blue-veined hand,
A weak white neck in velvet band,
With modest touch Aunt Susan plays
The tranquil 'Sheep May Safely Graze'
Of Bach, the tune she used to play,
On Sunday evenings years away,
To whiskered men of gentle sort
Who paid her strained and stately court.

The Landseer cattle on the wall,
The massy antlers in the hall,
The monumental two-year clock,
A faith in class as firm as rock,
And all the house, are just the same
As on the day the family came,
Firm barred against the new and strange
And devil-prompted thoughts of change.

Those gilt-edged shares will never drop,
But yearly yield a steady crop
To feed a world of certain grace
Where servants know their proper place.
The bombs that broke the windows here
Have not disturbed the atmosphere.

John Arlott (1914 - 1991)

Tea Party

"Do you believe love should be free?"
A raddled spinster said to me
One day in Bloomsbury at tea.
I looked into her eager eyes
Full of libidinous surmise
And thought, O God, can such things be?
I glanced across the heated room
Filled with conversational boom
And many a reputation's doom
And saw beyond the window pane
The pale October daylight wane…
And "No," I said with heartfelt gloom,
"I don't believe it ought to be,
I'd love another cup of tea".

Sheila Hackney

In Season

The man and woman on the blue and white
mug we have owned for so long
we can hardly remember
where we got it
or how

are not young. They are out walking in
a cobalt dusk under the odd azure of
apple blossom,
going towards each other with hands outstretched.

Suddenly this evening, for the first time,
I wondered *how will they find each other?*

For so long
they have been circling the small circumference
of an ironstone cup that they have forgotten,
if they ever really knew it, earth itself.

This top to bottom endlessly turning world
in which they only meet
each other meeting
each other
has no seasons, no intermission; and if

they do not know when light is rearranged
according to the usual celestial ordinance –
tides, stars, a less and later dusk –
and if they never noticed

the cotton edge of the curtains brightening earlier
on a spring morning after the clocks have changed
and changed again, it can only be

they have their own reasons, since
they have their own weather (a sudden fog,
tinted rain) which they have settled into

so that the kettle steam, the splash of new tea are
a sought-after climate endlessly folded
into a rinsed horizon.

Eavan Boland

Procedure

This tea, this cup of tea, made of leaves,
made of the leaves of herbs and absolute

almond blossom, this tea, is the interpreter
of almond, liquid touchstone which lets us
scent its true taste at last and with a bump,

in my case, takes me back to the yellow time
of trouble with blood tests, and cellular
madness, and my presence required

on the slab for the surgery, and all that mess
I don't want to comb through here because
it seems, honestly, a trifle now that steam

and scent and strength and steep and infusion
say thank you thank you thank you for the then, and now

Jo Shapcott